How to Deal

TAROT
FOR EVERYDAY LIFE

How to Deal

TAROT
FOR EVERYDAY LIFE

by Sami Main

illustrated by
Marisa de la Peña

HARPER
An Imprint of HarperCollinsPublishers

FOR TAMARA MAIN, AKA "MOMMO"

—S.M.

FOR MY FAMILY, ESPECIALLY MY MOTHER AND SISTER

—M.D.L.P.

TABLE OF CONTENTS

1

WELCOME TO THE CLUB!

Welcome to the world of tarot, my friends. Tarot is a way to get in touch with your powerful, mystical side. We all totally have one, and it's about time you tapped into yours.

Using the seventy-eight cards in a tarot deck, tarot readers attempt to predict and tell the future. You visit a reader for guidance if you want to send a question up to the universe and finally get it answered. (Good news is, by the end of this book, that tarot reader will be *you*!) By putting the cards in specific orders—we call them layouts—and then deciphering their message, you'll be able to answer any burning questions for yourself and for other curious folk around you. The magic of tarot is about judging a group of cards' meaning based on how they end up in a given layout.

I started teaching myself to read tarot cards a few years ago as a way to help answer big life questions. I had previously visited tarot readers and found them to be fascinating people with some kind of power of truth; one once told me I had an old soul, while another said I had lived eleven lifetimes and in each life I had been a healer or a mother figure.

Learning the skill of tarot meant that I could answer my own questions. Finally, I would have someone else to talk to about my life. And that someone was the universe. You know how you sometimes read your horoscope at the beginning of a month, just to prepare for what's coming up? It's the same thing with consulting the cards. Tarot is a way for me and my friends to get to the root of our problems. It's a bit like therapy. And if you leave yourself open to all the possible new experiences the tarot can teach you, I promise you won't regret it.

An important thing to remember is that the tarot will not give you a straight Y/N answer. The cards have lots of layers to them, which let you interpret them differently depending where they fall in a layout. On their own, every card has its individual meaning. Then these individual meanings inter-act once the cards are placed into a layout. (For example, as you'll learn later, if a Queen of Wands happens to fall across another card, that means the person that card represents is a challenge for you.) Each tarot reading you do uses the cards in a unique way. No two readings are ever the same—even if the same cards are drawn—because no two questions are the same and no two moments in life are the same.

I like to think of tarot as a weather forecast: it's predict-ing how things are going for you RIGHT NOW, but it's also aware that things can easily change. Tarot knows that fate is fluid. It's up to you to take matters into your own hands. If you find yourself going to multiple friends asking them what to do about the same problem, it means you're seeking out opinions, but you're not happy with what anyone has told you yet. That's a good sign that you should be asking the cards. Tarot can be an unbiased friend to you. Though, tarot has its limits, too: try not to ask about the exact same problem more than once a week. You can tell when the tarot is getting fed up with you.

For just a smidge of history: the first tarot cards showed

up in the 1400s as a playing card game in Italy. The usage of the cards slowly evolved into future-telling, and ultimately into how we use them today. The meanings you read nowadays are more modern than whatever medieval-pop-culture references those tarot readers used to make. And so this tarot book is a little different from others you might see: not only do the cards here have a female friendly energy that's missing from some of the older tarot decks, this book also has mini-exercises built into each section to help you lock in what you're learning. Neat!

In terms of finding the right deck for your tarot practice, there are lots of different styles out there. A tarot deck is similar to a set of playing cards, so you'll see cards like kings and queens. It might take a while until you find the perfect deck, so don't feel discouraged if you don't connect with the first one you get. Once you do find The One, make sure you keep it close so it can soak up your good energy. Do that by leaving it near your bed and shuffling through the cards every few days so they remember you. Tarot is just like a friend: you gotta check in with it every once in a while.

Before each reading, consider lighting a candle and

getting into a calm mind space. That might mean loading a Zen playlist, doing some yoga stretches, or meditating. How're you going to answer life's big questions if your own mind is stressy and cloudy? Tarot is all about vibes, so give it your best shot! I like lighting my peppermint candle and grabbing a nice mug of tea before sitting down to do a reading. As soon as I start laying out cards, my cat totally tries to play with them. If you're like me, then your cat, little sister, neighborhood ghost, or any other super determined nuisance will just hang out during your readings no matter what, so get used to it.

In the coming pages, you'll get to know the cards as they exist in two main categories: Minor Arcana and Major Arcana. The Minor Arcana are divided into the four suits: wands, cups, knives, and pentacles. Each suit has cards one through ten, and those number cards relate to everyday situations in your life like your hobbies, relationships, or career path. Suits also have four court cards—Pages, Knights, Queens, and Kings— and these will relate to the people in your life. If a court card comes up, try to think of someone you know— even if their gender doesn't match what's on the card—who fits that description. Meanwhile, the Major Arcana are tied to important milestones, big decisions, and the stages of your life; be sure to take them seriously if they show up in a reading. Major Arcana cards mean business.

As you go through the book, take a look at each card and its description and then practice using the exercises at the end of each section. Use the exercises when you're ready to start remembering the differences between all the cards and suits. Once you've gone through every card, I'll show you some reading layouts—how to place the cards in order to answer your and your friends' life questions. The intensity of your question determines the size of the layout; readings with fewer cards are for not-as-serious problems. Meanwhile, you should have as many as ten or more cards for your big-deal readings! Readings can be fun conversations between you, your friends, and the cards; the type of question decides the layout, which decides how the cards will speak back to you.

The most important rule of tarot: practice makes perfect. No one picks up a tarot deck and instantly understands how to interpret each and every card. It takes months to get familiar with your cards and their meanings. You'll grow more and more comfortable with your deck as you go and as it picks up vibes from you. Tarot is patient. And new meanings can jump out at you at any time, similar to how you reread a favorite book or rewatch a favorite movie and notice something different each time. At first, start by answering your own questions. Practice on yourself until you feel comfortable bringing your skills to your friends.

So what are you waiting for? Jump right in! The tarot's fine.

2

THE CARDS

WANDS

Wands are the cards of inspiration. Think of a match you strike to light a candle: *that's* a little wand, the beginning of something exciting and important. Wands also represent the hard work it takes to turn an idea into reality. Sometimes too much inspiration or motivation can feel like a bad thing, because you don't know where to put all that energy. With wands, there CAN be too much of a good thing. Other times, you feel like you're on the right track based on your gut feeling. With wands, you'll find your strength and understand what makes you feel confident.

ACE OF WANDS

All it takes is one idea to start something brilliant! This card represents the start of something awesome, an exciting beginning. Think of it as a flashlight—or, just as good, the flashlight app on your phone: with the Ace of Wands, you can start to recognize lots of possibilities all around you. If you see this card in a reading, get hyped! You're at the beginning of a cool and creative time.

TWO OF WANDS

Wands can inspire us, and they can also support us. These two wands are the bumpers on either side of your bowling lane: they'll keep pointing you toward your goal, while making sure you're staying on the best path possible. Two is an even, balanced number, and you won't feel overwhelmed by the options in front of you. Treat yourself right, and you can totally make that metaphorical strike waiting for you at the end of the lane. When you see this card, remember how strong you feel when you're at your most focused.

THREE OF WANDS

It's the #squadgoals card! The ultimate card of support! Where would you be without your key team? This card reminds you of all your friends and family members who've helped along the way. If this card comes up, maybe it's time for you to remember your friends. Lean on them (when you're not strong . . .). Lean on them, but no need to let go of your own opinions. Your buddies have helped you along, but you're still independent and can make your own choices. Just celebrate the advice and help they've given.

FOUR OF WANDS

Congrats! Let the good times roll! A lot of the wands cards want you to stay on track toward your goals. AKA lots of hard work. Luckily, this card tells you the hardest work is behind you. Take a moment to breathe deep—like, yoga deep. Recognize how far you've come. Maybe a cool party in your honor is in order. Or you're about to deliver a killer presentation you've worked extra hard on. If you see this card, give yourself a pat on the back (and be sure to thank the people who helped you get to this point).

FIVE OF WANDS

Whoa. What's up lately? Feeling scattered? This card relates directly to our energies and how confused we get when we don't know what to do with all that inspiration. There's always a ton going on in our lives, and we often feel pulled in many directions. Maybe you have a lot of projects you want to work on, but aren't convinced about which ones deserve your attention. This card is a reminder to chill. You might feel all over the place for the moment, and you just need to figure out exactly where to point your wands.

SIX OF WANDS

Don't forget to keep your eyes on the prize. Stay focused on what's ahead. That's what this card is all about. Keep moving forward instead of looking back at your past. Sure, there might've been some hiccups, but you've learned from them. You can—and will!—succeed. Keep what you need, and let go of the rest.

SEVEN OF WANDS

It's all on you! Sounds totally scary being the one in charge or being super responsible. It's time to rely on no one but yourself. See how much of a leader you can become by digging down deep and recognizing your inner strength. When this card comes around, remember everything you've already accomplished and how awesome you are.

EIGHT OF WANDS

Change is on its way, my friend. All eight of these wands are pointed toward your goal, whatever that may be. Something swift is now in the air, and I'm not talking about Taylor. See how the wands are all heading in the same direction? So are you! This card is pointing toward some recent clarity that has guided you, so stay the course. Try not to fight this strong new direction.

NINE OF WANDS

Hear that huffing and puffing? That's the sound of YOU doing tons of hard work. Dang. These metaphorical wands—think of them as challenges—have continued to stack up in front of you like some kind of treadmill from hell. You're totally tired and ready to give up. Each wand is another task or responsibility you've taken on. But you can't quit yet! You're super close to making it. Think about your journey so far, and use that to push yourself over the finish line. This card is all about past struggles being in the PAST, and how you don't need to let them clog your mind.

TEN OF WANDS

That's a load of wands, my friend. Apparently, plenty of things have been weighing you down, both physically and mentally. Does it feel like you've made progress but don't have a lot to show for it? Like, when you do all the work on a math problem and still get it wrong? That sucks. It feels like you're so close to your goal, yet it's still JUST out of reach. This card wants you to decide if you're making it too hard for yourself and you need to walk away, or if you need to tough it out a bit longer and see it through. The most important thing is simply to decide, once and for all, how to handle it.

PAGE OF WANDS

The Page of Wands is a person brimming with creative passion. They've got lots of neat ideas at all times, even if they're not positive which one they want to focus on. And they certainly know how to turn a boring party into one everyone will be talking about the next day! But they can come across as selfish because they're so into everything they've got going on. Just like with every court card, if this card comes up in a reading, someone who fits this description is involved.

KNIGHT OF WANDS

Well, well, well. What do we have here? Someone who's so confident, they always seem to say the right things at the right time. This card represents a bit of a charming daredevil. They love adventure and getting started on new beginnings. Don't try to slow this person down or get in their way; they're not here to tussle with dillydallyers!

QUEEN OF WANDS

Think of this person as a more mature version of the Page of Wands: they're organized yet creative; they know exactly what they want to be doing, and they can get it done with ease. Being the Queen of Wands looks effortless. People are drawn to this person just to be around their comforting and driven energy.

KING OF WANDS

A bit of mystery, a dash of charm, a pinch of pizazz. The King of Wands is someone quite happy with who they are. The King of Wands loves coming up with creative ideas that behave logically; think of them like the one person in a group project who figures out the perfect compromise to get everyone to work together. A person like this card is super creative and is good to turn to with your problems—you'll find them to be compassionate and a good listener.

1 *List your two best friends and what makes them your best friends. Together, plus you, they're who make up your Three of Wands. These are your go-to people for when you're in a tough spot and you need a hand up or a hand to hold. Whenever the Three of Wands comes up, remember it represents this support group.*

2 *Who's the Queen of Wands in your life? Who's got it all figured out? (They probably only look like they do—but still...) Take a minute to write down the qualities you admire in them. What makes them seem so effort-less? Because that's what makes a good Queen of Wands.*

3 *Jot down your goals in life. Think big! Write as many goals as you want, then pick the one you want to accomplish first. Now write down what your Ace of Wands—your spark, your inspiration, your starting point—is for that goal. What's the first step that you can realistically take to make that come true?*

4 Sometimes we take on too many things and feel scattered. It happens! Think of a time when you felt that way and list out all the problems you were dealing with. All those were examples of too many wands weighing you down. The lesson here is prioritizing better next time.

5 *Think of the person in your life who's super fun but maybe doesn't have their stuff figured out yet. They've always got a good idea, but sometimes way too many of them all at once! That's the Page of Wands, a totally creative person who maybe doesn't have everything nailed down. No judgment, but list some of the personality traits of that person.*

CUPS

C ups are all about emotions, baby. Think of them like the place deep inside where you hide all your feelings, both good and bad. They're where you keep your internal happiness rainbows. Just make sure your cup doesn't runneth too far over. . . .

ACE OF CUPS

Raise a glass to YOU, my friend! This card represents the start of something special, something that will really make you feel good. It could mean a new relationship is on your horizon, or maybe that one nagging stressful problem will finally solve itself. Whatever it is, get ready! This cup may be empty—but not for long. Cheers!

TWO OF CUPS

Picture the kinds of situations where you see two cups sitting together: could be a couple on a date or two friends meeting up for coffee. Either way, it's better together! The Two of Cups wants to tell you about a big, exciting relationship or friendship that's about to start. And it's one that's gonna last, not just a ship passing in the night. If you see this card, look at the people around you. One of them is here for the long haul.

THREE OF CUPS

It takes two to tango, but three to party! This is a card about celebration. You and your team deserve to recognize just how special you are together. Who are your besties? The ones you can always call on? The ones who will sing all the words to the *Gilmore Girls* theme song with you? That's who this card is about. If no one quite comes to mind, then keep hope alive; they're right around the corner. Does this card remind you of the Three of Wands? Well, those were your support group; these are the friends you reach out to when you're ready to celebrate.

FOUR OF CUPS

You may project an air of someone who's got it all figured out. But YOU know what's really going on deep down, where you feel less than confident. It's important to be genuine with the people in your life. This card wants you to go after what makes you happy—but don't be afraid to let other people in and let them see who you truly are.

FIVE OF CUPS

Not a great card to get, but try to see it as a helpful warning rather than a scare tactic. Take a step back. This card can tell things are gonna get real rough, if they haven't already. Do what you can to avoid the pit of sadness. And if you find yourself already in that hole, don't beat yourself up even more.

SIX OF CUPS

Dive into your memories! No, not the embarrassing moments from middle school. Instead, think about what made you feel right as rain and super happy way back when. Channel that now! Embrace your past. Maybe an old friend will come around and help you—let them! This card is all about remembering what makes you happy and wrapping it around you like a blanket.

SEVEN OF CUPS

Wait, what? Hold up. Things are a little tricky and confusing. Left is right, black is white, up is down. Life is trying to throw you for a loop. This card knows that, sometimes, people are out to get you, and it wants you to be aware of it. How can you avoid these potholes? Take a step back. Remember your true goals, and don't let anything trip you up. Rise above it all by waiting a sec to let things sort themselves out instead of getting stuck in the middle of a mess.

EIGHT OF CUPS

How can I put this gently? There's nothing left here for you anymore, honey. It's time to move on. Think of this as an opportunity to start fresh, leave the past in the past. Trust me, it's not going to do you any good to keep dwelling on it. Maybe a no good love has been dragging you along for the ride and you're ready to be on your own. Think of these eight cups as empty. They're done, and so are you with this nonsense.

NINE OF CUPS

Take a deep breath. RELAX. This card knows that great blessings are coming your way, from health to relationships and maybe even to your wallet. Hold your head high, and act like the awesome person you are. Soak it all in! You deserve a break.

TEN OF CUPS

High fives all around! This is one of the happiest cards in the whole deck of tarot. There is such joy in your life now. Or perhaps it's right around the corner waiting for you. Whenever it arrives, be sure to appreciate that joy. People love to see you this happy; it makes them happy, too! Trust this feeling of positivity, and let it show!

PAGE OF CUPS

The person this card represents enjoys bringing up their feelings but doesn't always know how to best communicate them. Use this person and court card as a reminder to express yourself. It's important to say what's on your mind before it's too late! No one wants to be the person who waited too long to ask out their crush and missed out.

KNIGHT OF CUPS

This card represents someone very charming, very sure of themselves. The Knight of Cups also represents someone a little dark and mysterious. Whoever this is, they probably have a few secrets inside and are turning inward to deal with the problems.

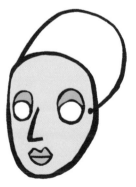

QUEEN OF CUPS

Such a breath of fresh air! Welcome to a very insightful person, someone who's really in touch with themselves. Definitely trust their intuition. But remember: don't try to push this sensitive person too far. They can get very defensive very quickly, including when it comes to their friends. This is a mother-hen type.

KING OF CUPS

This card, and person, is all about the family. They want to support everyone, which means they might get a little lost in the flow. They don't always stand out in a crowd. Either way, they have a lovely open mind and they use it quite fairly. Go to them for advice, but don't forget to lend them a shoulder when they need it (even if they don't ask)!

1 Put yourself in the shoes of the Page of Cups. What's something you wish you could express to someone? It doesn't have to be a huge secret. Maybe there's someone you've been dying to tell off, or maybe your sibling has been super annoying lately. Maybe you want to tell your crush how you really feel. Take this space to acknowledge what you need to get off your chest.

2 *Keep a feelings journal. For the whole day, or until you run out of room, write down every emotion you have. We have a lot of emotions, all the time, and sometimes more than one at once! Be patient with yourself—and others—and remember that we're all dealing with plenty of feels.*

3 *Who—or what—do you need to let go of? Make room for something way happier to come into your life, like the Eight of Cups wants you to.*

4 The Ten of Cups is kind of like the best shindig you've ever thrown—your graduation party mixed with your Sweet 16. Play Pinterest for a minute, and list out what would make the perfect party.

5 *Who are your go-to party people? When you're ready to celebrate, who do you turn to? Decide what about those friends makes them your Three of Cups.*

KNIVES

TEAR PROOF

KNIVES

In some tarot decks, knives are also called swords, just in case that issue comes up in your tarot journey. Whatever they're called, these are sharp, pointy truths. Knives represent your honest thoughts and how dangerous those can be when not wielded appropriately.

ACE OF KNIVES

This card is your "aha!" moment. Hold on to this feeling, because it's an exciting one! Suddenly, you've got a lot of clarity. That's great! Maybe you finally know what you want to be when you get older. In tarot, knives are related to your brainpower and thought processes, and those are important to stay connected with.

TWO OF KNIVES

Ugh, great. You're not the best at making decisions. (But, really, who is?!) You've reached a stalemate with yourself, and that's never helpful. It's like you've been blindfolded and you can't see which direction is the right one to go in. Are you getting in your own way again? Snap out of it! Even if there's something you hate to admit, it's time to move past that. This card wants you to wake up and acknowledge what's really going on.

THREE OF KNIVES

This card deals with a lot of deep emotions, and they're not all good ones. If knives represent our mind, this card is about your head and your heart having a tough time working together. Has someone been lying to you and you just found out? Has your BFF started dating your secret crush, even though they promised not to? That sucks, really. This card means you should wait a minute before acting impulsively on your hurt feelings.

FOUR OF KNIVES

With so much going on around you, this card reminds you to pause and breathe. That's the only way you'll have the strength to move forward and not make the wrong moves. You never know who you can truly trust, so before you spill all your secrets to the wrong friend, take a moment. Pause, think, reflect.

FIVE OF KNIVES

Those weird feelings that have been floating around you for a while? Here's the bad news: it's all your fault. Sorry! You wanted too much too soon, and now you're questioning everything. Try not to worry about this a ton (obviously easier said than done). You can fix it, you just have to slow down first. And worrying about a problem won't make it any easier to solve. This card wants you to learn how to become the master of your own thoughts before trying to move forward.

SIX OF KNIVES

Remember all those negative thoughts you had when you were pitying yourself? Banish them. You're not entirely out of this particular jam, but you're on your way. This card is here to remind you that hope exists, so embrace it! Use your thoughts for good; they're some of the most powerful tools you have. Be kind to yourself. Take a breather.

SEVEN OF KNIVES

Are you hiding something from your best friend? Are you hiding something from yourself? Is someone hiding something from YOU? A whole lot of secrecy's afoot! Knowledge is power, and someone isn't being told all the key info. It's time to figure it out or fess up—or face the consequences.

EIGHT OF KNIVES

You seem stuck! Not a fun feeling. But maybe YOU are the one holding YOU back? Think about it. It's time to recognize what you want to be doing, and don't let anything distract you from reaching those goals. You feel trapped between a rock and a hard place, and it's time to start making moves, even if that's scary. Pick a direction, any direction, instead of no direction at all—you'll figure out if it's the right choice pretty quickly.

NINE OF KNIVES

You might need more rest—the kind of rest that comes from being at peace with yourself. Feeling guilty or depressed is totally natural, and this card is all about those thoughts you've been using against yourself. We all get into funks. Try not to blame yourself for too long, though. You're only human! Maybe it's time you reached out to friends and family who know how to support you during this tough time.

TEN OF KNIVES

Yikes! This is what happens when the power of knives turns against us. This card is about a big helping of self-destruction with a side of rock bottom. Sometimes we beat ourselves up too much—but why should we? Doesn't the whole world do that for us all the time? Now, pick yourself up, brush yourself off, and put your best face forward. There's a hopeful horizon once you look beyond your problems. This is the only time that a ten in tarot will seem so dramatic, but it's because our own thoughts are sometimes our worst enemies.

PAGE OF KNIVES

This person is totally open and honest, even though their truth can be a little hard to hear. They're super observant, all the time, forever. Like an elephant, they also never forget what they notice. And it can be hard for them to turn it off! Useful skill when you're bonding over memories, but not very cool when you want people to forget your most embarrassing moments.

KNIGHT OF KNIVES

The Knight of Knives is very determined, focused, and goal oriented, so their perspective can be super helpful. Plus, they're very intelligent (as are all court cards associated with knives in tarot). Sometimes, they can be too go-go-go, so don't try to keep up if you don't have the right kind of stamina.

QUEEN OF KNIVES

As a good listener, the Queen of Knives is also very smart in their chosen field. Maybe this is your friend who knows everything covered in your classes even though it's all Greek to you. This person is perceptive, so they probably know when you need help before you're ready to ask. It's important for this person to be patient when giving criticism, though, because it could easily come across as too harsh.

KING OF KNIVES

A very fair person, but that fairness can turn into a negative pretty quick: they can take themselves so emotionally out of a situation that they seem cold and unfeeling. Oops! They don't INTEND for that to happen, it just does. Either way, they're very respected in all friend groups, and you might ask them for help making decisions. At least they're responsible, even if they might come across as unkind.

1 Write down three things people wouldn't know about you by just looking at you. Those are some knives, so use them wisely.

2 *Think about a time when your head disagreed with your heart. Maybe you had a huge crush on someone you knew would be bad for you. Imagine or sketch out your own Three of Knives card to help remind you of that time. Then remember how much it sucked.*

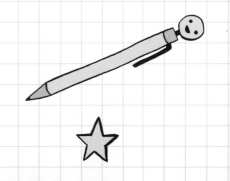

3 *What's been an "aha!" moment for you lately? Did you make a big decision recently? That moment you knew exactly what to do: that's your Ace of Knives!*

4 *Think of your lowest low. It's no fun, I know. But your Ten of Knives moment is your bottomest of rock bottoms. Instead of dwelling on it, though, list everything you did to get out of that black hole.*

5 The tricky part about knives is that they can turn on us super quickly. The point of this exercise is to help you collect your thoughts so they don't come back to bite you later. Get in this habit if you want to control these knives a little more easily. Use this space to write down everything that pops into your head while taking some deep breaths. Meditating can be hard, but it's okay if your thoughts wander. They're allowed.

Pentacles

PENTACLES

Pentacles are the fourth suit in tarot. These magical objects/talismans represent all things physical in your world—this can mean money, your home life, or even anything you've bought online lately. Other suits are about your thoughts or feelings, whereas this one's about things outside your personality, like your belongings or career goals.

ACE OF PENTACLES

Something delightful is about to start! Pentacles represent money and other material goodies (even your health and your home), and aces signal beginnings. So, while nothing may be happening right now, you should be doing your darnedest to put your best foot forward for the future. Maybe you need to buckle down and prep now to do well on something later, or skip this month's Spotify subscription to save for a bigger splurge. Either way, a good thing is brewing....

TWO OF PENTACLES

Look at you, supergirl! This card knows you're the master of balance, change, and taking things as they come. You know that once you've got this situation under control and can move ahead, new things are fun things! Embrace the change that needs to happen, so that even better things can enter your life. Are you trying to juggle new extracurriculars or a new job with other commitments? This card just wants you to be as balanced as possible.

THREE OF PENTACLES

Listen, you know you're awesome. But you also know you didn't get to be this awesome all by yourself. Think about your besties, or even your family members, who helped you along the way. Remember that as you set new goals; think about how you'll achieve those things and who can help you. We all get by with a little help from our friends, so don't be afraid to lean on folks. This card represents the cool things you can achieve when you have a team by your side.

FOUR OF PENTACLES

The Four of Pentacles can either be a comforting card or a warning card; you'll have to see how it fits within your reading. It's a well-meaning card and doesn't want you to worry. On one hand, it's showing definite stability when it comes to your finances or your home life. On the other hand, it could be telling you not to be TOO controlling when it comes to your possessions. If you're feeling stable, remember to share your knowledge or tips with others. There's no need to hold on too tightly to material goods or to be selfish. Has your BFF been asking to borrow your cute new top? Just say yes! Prove how fair and secure you are with your stuff. This card supports you. Just remember to stay humble to avoid any trouble.

FIVE OF PENTACLES

Cheer up, buttercup. This card represents our sads. You're worried about something, or someone. Have your friends been leaving you behind lately? Are you worried about how worried you've been? That's not helping anyone! Of course you're allowed to be in a funk for a little while, but take a moment to realize WHAT has been making you feel this way. Maybe losing that bracelet wasn't such a big deal after all. Deep breaths. Things probably aren't as bad as you think. There's a lot of power in that noggin of yours, so put it to good use.

SIX OF PENTACLES

Things are finally going your way! All the hard work you've put into your job or classes or both is finally about to pay off. Remember: once you feel secure, you should try to give a little back to your friends and family. The more you give, the more you'll get. No one likes a Scrooge. Take a moment to celebrate everything you've worked toward, then get ready to enjoy it with your pals! Don't hog all the joy.

SEVEN OF PENTACLES

Now that the period of hard work is behind you, you're bound to find yourself with a few questions about whether it was all worth it. Who cares if you're the top of your class if you didn't make time to have a social life—does that make you a total failure or a real winner? Does any of it matter? Try not to dwell on things too much. Recognize your hard work, lean in to your success, then get ready to move on. Sometimes, it's all right not to look back.

EIGHT OF PENTACLES

I t's all you. You're at the top of your game, you're the cream of the crop. Maybe you're the one everyone looks up to—it's for a good reason! You've honed your skills. And if it feels like you're nowhere close to being a pro, maybe it's time to start a new hobby that will allow you to get there. This card wants to remind you of how good you are at what you do. Look back at all you've accomplished and be proud!

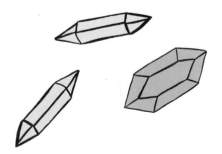

NINE OF PENTACLES

You're basically on cloud nine, pun intended. You're feeling comfortable enough in your success to enjoy it. You're near the end of a project, and you're ready to relax. You've earned it! Kick up your feet, grab a jar of Nutella and a spoon, and let yourself chill out a little. You're allowed to be happy! It took ya long enough. This card is all about feeling satisfied and at home with yourself.

TEN OF PENTACLES

This card will show up when you're on the right track, or when you're done with a tough project or tough time in your life. Hopefully the journey was worth every bump in the road, now that you've reached such a happy place. Look around you; are others struggling to keep up with your brilliance? Lend a helping hand! Think how much you would've liked some help on your way to the top, and pay it forward.

PAGE OF PENTACLES

The Page of Pentacles is the quiet kind, and there's nothing wrong with that! This person enjoys a little hard work, even if that work takes place behind the scenes without any glory. They're super responsible, but try not to rely on them all the time. They'll put up with it . . . only for so long. This is a very detail-oriented person who can be super independent.

KNIGHT OF PENTACLES

The loyal Knight of Pentacles would be great to have on your side in an argument. Of course, that's only once you get to know them, which might take some time and effort. Think of the quiet person in the cafeteria. They could be a great friend, but you'd never know unless, and until, you get them talking. Just watch out: that loyal intensity can morph into stubbornness in certain situations.

QUEEN OF PENTACLES

This person excels in the home; it's like everything they touch turns to Martha Stewart gold! Extremely confident in their abilities, the Queen of Pentacles can solve any problem that comes up. They're the friend who always carries Purell in their purse or packs an extra bag of pretzels for lunch. Sometimes, this person needs to be needed, which isn't always fun to be around. But at the end of the day, they make you feel like family.

KING OF PENTACLES

A patient and kind person. Does that make them a little boring? Perhaps a little . . . but sometimes boring is good. There won't be any drama with this person, and we could all use more friends like that. They want stability, always, and that makes them calm and nice to be around. This person can tend to be passionate on the inside.

1 *What makes you happy? How do you measure success? It doesn't have to be an amount of money, but maybe you like winning at sports or maybe you like getting your writing published. Think about what you value, and that's what pentacles means to you.*

2 *Sharing is caring. List some of the nicest things your friends or family have done for you. Remember how happy that made you? Be sure to do what you can to let others feel that joy, too. (Not constantly, because then you'd be exhausted! But hold the door for a stranger every now and then—it won't hurt you.)*

3 *What would you do if you won the lottery? Write or draw what you would buy or do with all those winnings.*

4 What piece of advice do you wish you'd received the last time you were going through a rough patch? Write it down, so you can remember the next time you see the Ten of Pentacles. It's nice to help others feel as happy as you do.

5 *What are two things you're juggling right now? That's what you're dealing with when the Two of Pentacles comes up. Whatever's on your mind that you might feel torn between, that's where you need to find a balance. Write it down here to work through it.*

153

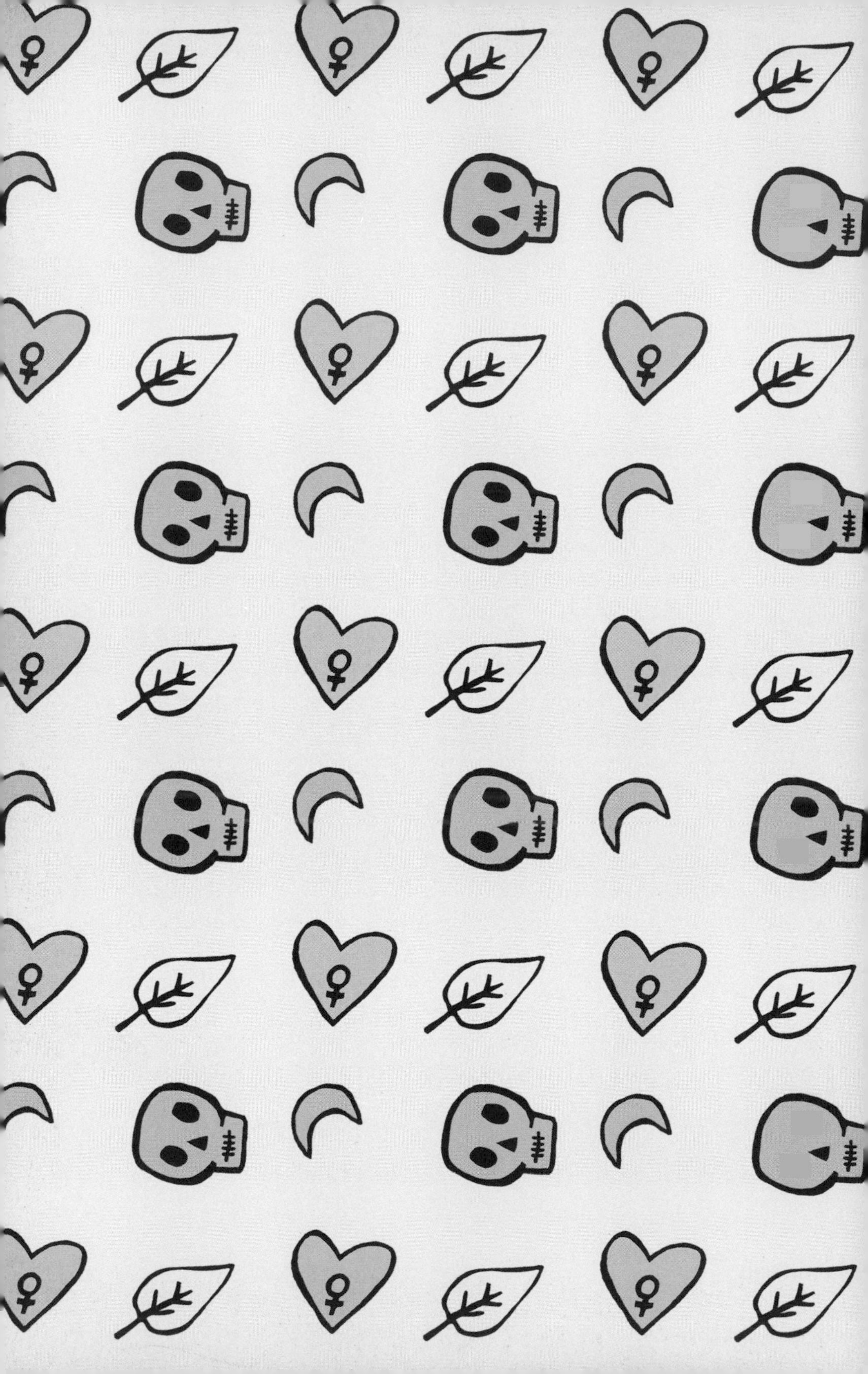

MAJOR ARCANA

The Major Arcana is a special part of the tarot deck; unlike the Minor Arcana, which has four suits and fourteen cards in each suit, the Major Arcana has only one of each card for a total of twenty-two. When these cards show up in a reading, they're calling your attention to a big life moment or milestone. This means they are slightly more important than the Minor Arcana cards, which deal with day-to-day situations. Not that Major Arcana cards should take over and dominate a reading if and when they appear; you still need to look at the layout as a whole without focusing on one or two cards. Think of the Major Arcana like this: they're about major (ahem) life themes that need addressing—relationships, personal demons and downfalls, key decisions—so, naturally, you're going to want to perk if they come calling.

THE FOOL

This is the one and only time it's okay to be called a fool. The Fool is excited to start on a new adventure, and you should be, too! Can it be scary to take those first steps on a new project or journey? Of course. Try to find joy in the unknown.

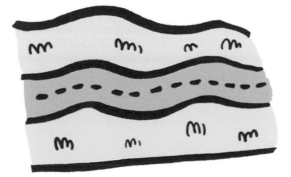

THE MAGICIAN

Get going! What good is a magician who doesn't show off their skills? No one's asking you to be like that one guy who always tries to impress everyone, but this is a card all about owning your talents. Realize what you have to offer and put it to good use. It's all within you! You can do so much already—don't be afraid to use your abilities.

THE HIGH PRIESTESS

The High Priestess is one of the strongest female energies in the entire deck, and she's here to look out for you. She represents our inner mysteries and curiosities. Notice how STILL she is. She's found a sense of control and peacefulness; she's got all the power when it comes to our dream worlds. When you see this card, take a moment to consider what's going on behind the scenes of what you're asking about. Is there something hidden that isn't being addressed? Perhaps you should try to find out, rather than ignore it. The High Priestess knows every secret.

THE EMPRESS

If the High Priestess is all about the power of secrets and stillness, then the Empress is all about creation and intuition. The Empress is a maternal figure, like the person in your friend group who always knows people will need extra snacks or Tylenol. Because the Empress is a card about nurturing your spirit, it's also a card about nature. It's the voice inside your head that's centuries old, like your gut instincts. If this card shows up, you're either plenty in touch with that side of yourself or you need to reconnect stat. If it's the latter, tap into that gut instinct and help yourself out.

THE EMPEROR

The Emperor, masculine in energy, is all about stability. This is a sturdy and dependable person who will always be there for you. The Emperor is someone with goals and structure and might be a good example for you to follow. OR maybe this person IS you! Stick to your gumption and trust your decisions. Whereas the Empress is a person guided by their intuition, the Emperor is guided more by logic.

THE HIEROPHANT

Hierophant is an old-world term for *priest*. Though this card doesn't necessarily point toward religion, it represents a teacher or mentor figure in your life. Have you been needing extra guidance somewhere? Find someone who can get you going in the right direction. Maybe you've been wanting to join a new club or start a new hobby—what are you waiting for? Sign up for a class and start learning a whole new skill. Don't be afraid to shake things up a bit.

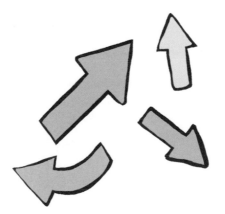

THE LOVERS

Yes, the Lovers. The Lovers is all about those people in any kind of relationship with you (not just someone who's your romantic love). You're in relationships with your friends, your family, and, you guessed it, also those you're dating. If this card shows up, it's pointing at an important relationship or partnership in your life. Maybe something new and exciting is about to start, so keep an extra pair of your cutest jeans or your most serious blazer around just in case. A partnership could be just what you need.

THE CHARIOT

Think back to the last time you performed really well. Or to a time when you placed well in a competition. That golden, bubbly feeling in your chest? That's pride, and that's confidence, and that's SO GREAT. That's your Chariot. Your Chariot is where you turn when you need some pep in your step. Stick with your Chariot if you want to go far. If this card comes up, it's trying to remind you of the direction you want to be headed.

STRENGTH

Dorothy had the power to get herself home from Oz all along! Her red shoes were her Strength card. Sometimes you're more powerful than you ever realized. Maybe we're not told often enough just how strong we are, so consider this your reminder: you've got the control, you've got the smarts, you've got the passion. Strength doesn't mean you go around beating people up; it means you know when to make your voice heard or when to hang back and wait.

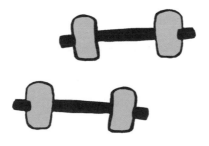

THE HERMIT

Ah, the Hermit. Does it sound like a sad card at first? It may seem gloomy and lonely, like when you spend the weekend on your couch in sweatpants. Well, the Hermit is here to remind you to pause and check in with yourself. Through meditation and reflection, you'll more clearly see the path you should be following. Sitting quietly with yourself and your thoughts can sound awful, but sometimes we need to look inward before we can move outward. The Hermit wants to be your guide, to illuminate what's ahead of you. Sometimes we can only achieve that by finding some inner peace. So take a minute to chill before making a big decision.

WHEEL OF FORTUNE

No, not like the TV game show. (Unless that show is some kind of grand metaphor for life.) THIS Wheel of Fortune is all about fate. Without you even worrying about it, the world is in motion and is already doing a lot of work for us. Sometimes, you just gotta let the universe take care of things. There's something bigger than yourself at work behind the scenes. You can't stop the wheel, you can't change the wheel, you just gotta let the wheel do its thing and hope for the best. Sometimes this is a relief, so that you don't have to do all the worrying all the time. But sometimes, it can seem like the wheel is a little bit unfair. That's life!

JUSTICE

Some tough choices are heading your way, so get ready to weigh your decision. This card reminds you that any decision you make could easily come back to affect you. Your actions have all kinds of repercussions in the future, for yourself and everyone else. Try to think carefully before taking any actions. You don't have to be scared of your choices, but now's the time to remember that balance is important.

THE HANGED WOMAN

Flipping yourself totally upside down, as this card suggests, might seem like a huge deal and a little scary! But here's the thing: you're not perfect. Okay, maybe you're CLOSE to perfect. But we all, from time to time, need a shift of perspective. Don't be afraid to ask around for other points of view, because you never know what you're missing out on. This change of perspective won't always be easy, though. Admitting that you need to see things differently can come after a hard realization. Don't pressure yourself, or anyone else, as you seek this out. Let it go. Let it all go. This change has to come, and it'll be good for you in the end.

DEATH

I'll wait until you pick the book back up. Scary, right? But seeing the Death card in a reading isn't an omen of doom. Here's what it REALLY means: it's time to move on. There's something going on that is no longer serving you in a helpful way, so you need to get rid of it. Something new can't start until something old gets the heave-ho. How can you squeeze a new sweater into your closet if those old styles that don't even fit anymore are still in there? Get rid of the past so you can move on!

TEMPERANCE

Temperance in tarot is here to renew your spirit. Find a fresh take on life by leaning into the balance the universe is presenting to you. Beyond just your neighborhood yoga class, balance can mean you're the peacemaker in your friend group for a little while—the one who's trying to make everything okay. Part of creating balance means compromising. Sweetness and harmony are good things to go after in life, and occasionally that means developing a give-and-take with your wants and needs. This card recognizes the importance of finding the middle ground.

THE DEVIL

Yeah, so this doesn't mean the ACTUAL devil. Here, it's the representation of something not great. He's trying to showcase the icky parts of your life that need to be pushed away. Do you have bad habits that keep causing problems? Is there someone in your life who continues bringing negative energy to you? This card isn't trying to blame anybody; it just wants you to acknowledge that some bad energy is floating around. Take stock and see what could be eliminated from your life to bring more joy around you.

THE TOWER

In traditional tarot decks, the Tower refers to the Tower of Babel from the Christian Bible. Tl;dr: an entire society falls apart due to mass miscommunication. Let's bring that lesson into today's world. Miscommunication is everywhere! Especially over text or social media. It's super easy to, say, rip someone apart for their tone in a group text. This card is a warning about that. Be as clear as possible when you're talking with absolutely anyone, just in case. If something is breaking down in your life right now, and you didn't see it coming, then this card is a reminder that things can be rebuilt. Damage doesn't need to last forever. But learn from whatever caused those problems instead of just bouncing away from them.

THE STAR

Look up! See all those stars? There are tons of them, just as there are tons of possibilities. The Star is a card of hope; it's here to remind you that there's plenty else going on in the world beyond your joys and fears, and that's a good thing. Everyone else is just as confused or as grateful as you are, and we're all connected by that dang starry sky. Let it relax you a bit.

THE MOON

Whenever you see the Moon come up in tarot, even if it's in the background of the art on other cards, just remember: secrets. The Moon is always around when you're dreaming; that's when your true self peeks out, including the things you won't admit to yourself in the light of day. Your dreams and daydreams let you reach new levels of creativity, like when your best ideas come to you in the shower. The Moon is all about your true self, even the hidden stuff. Accept your Moon side before it leaks out when you least expect it.

THE SUN

S oak it all in. The sun gives us energy and life and hope (compare your mood in the winter to how you feel when you see the first signs of spring)—and so should this card. Without the sun, we don't have anything. Let this card remind you to take care of yourself, like you would a garden. You need water and sunshine just like anyone else, and that's a glorious thing. Make sure you feed your soul. This is the tarot card of self-care and how good you deserve to feel. Aim for that.

JUDGMENT

This is still a no-judgment zone, don't worry. In tarot, this card wants to release you of the fear of judgment. Accept blame if you need to, but then move on. Holding grudges against the person who always seems to be ahead just ends up making YOU feel bad. Try to let go of those petty feelings (which are totally normal to feel) before they get stuck inside you for too long. Making atonements and forgiving people, even yourself, are a huge part of growing up. Be the bigger person before worse judgment can fall on you.

THE WORLD

goals. Because this card is at the end of the Major Arcana, it represents the completion of something. The World is all about what you're aiming for in life. It's what completes you. The World is what your life will look like when you're at 100 percent happiness. Not always super easy to get to, right? In a perfect world, of course you'd get amazing marks, have awesome friends, and excel in whatever brings you joy. But we're not always there. And if you're not there, it's important to know what you need to rock your World. Think for a bit about what it takes to make you happy.

1 *Think of the various skills you possess. What are you the best at? Or what are you just now getting good at? It's okay if your list is short. This is who you are as the Magician. These traits are what count for that card.*

2 *The Moon holds all your dreams and secrets. What's a dream you've never told anyone about a life goal you have? Even if you don't write it down, it's important to know what you're aiming for.*

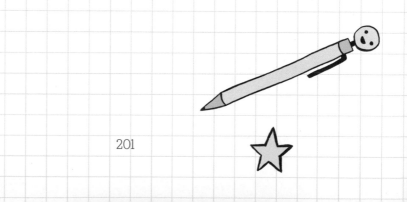

3 *Use this space to write or draw what your Chariot looks and feels like. Tap into your inner confidence and know what makes you glow.*

4 *We've all got bad habits lying around. What are some things you've been meaning to get out of your life? Do you bite your nails? Do you talk behind people's backs? Those bad habits are what the Devil card wants you to recognize.*

5 *Think back on the Lovers card. Who are some people in your life that are your best buddies or fab partners in crime? (This can include the person you're dating, too.) Each person is an important part of your life, even if they play very different roles.*

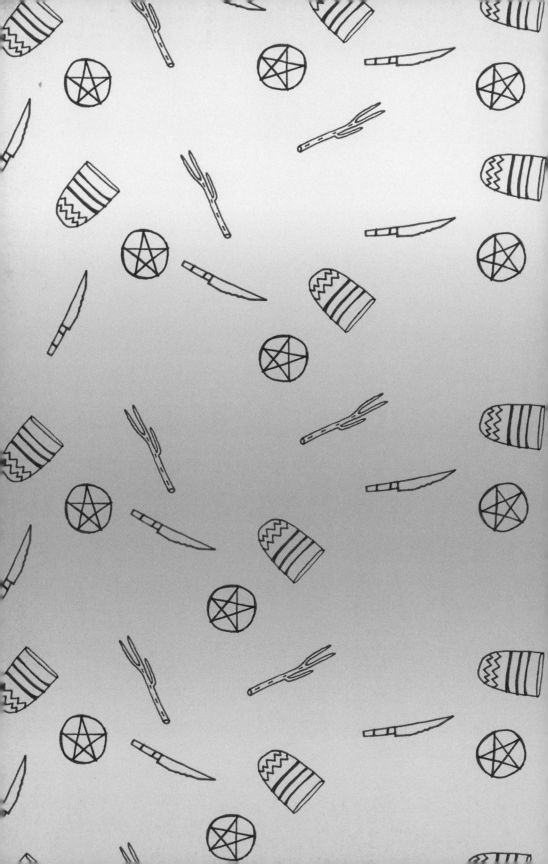

3

TAROT TRAINING

Congratulations! You've made it through all seventy-eight cards. Phew. I know it's quite a bit to take in. Feel free to go back and review the cards at any point along your tarot journey. Even during readings, it's always fine to check the card descriptions as a refresher.

When you feel ready, here are a few general exercises before you get into layouts.

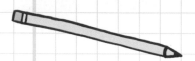

1 *Match these four words with the suit of tarot that they best fit by drawing a line across the page.*

INSPIRATION   KNIVES

MATERIALS   CUPS

TRUTH   WANDS

EMOTIONS   PENTACLES

2 Can tarot tell the future for you? Or is it more of a forecasting system? Write down how you approach your tarot practice. Think about how you would explain it to a friend you're doing a reading for.

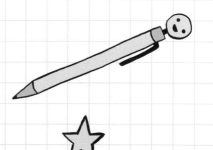

3 *What's your favorite tarot card? Is there one in particular that speaks to you? Write about why it's your favorite.*

4 *Summarize the difference between the Minor and Major Arcana.*

4

LAYOUTS

Now that you've learned about all seventy-eight cards, here are some layouts that will help you answer your own questions and questions from your friends. As a reminder, the size of the layout you choose should be in line with how big/important the question is. Have fun playing with each layout, and remember, it's best to practice on yourself before reaching out to friends.

Before you start a reading, here are some ways you can get your space into the tarot mood:

Put down a cloth where you plan to lay out the cards. This could be a favorite scarf or other special fabric that you use to wrap your tarot cards in.

Light a candle (not too strong/smelly!), and make sure it's not too close to your cards . . . just in case.

Shuffle your entire deck multiple times, while really letting yourself rest in the moment. Focus on the question you're asking as you shuffle. If the reading is for a friend, have them repeat their question aloud a couple of times to lock in what they're really asking. And feel free to ask your friend any quick follow-ups about what they're hoping to find out, just so it informs your reading even more. Make sure the cards stay in the same direction, so when you're ready to deal them out, you won't mess with upside-down cards.

 After shuffling, have your friend cut the deck into three

different piles of roughly equal size. They get to put those three piles back together into one. This way, BOTH of your energies are with the cards.

    With a layout in mind, start dealing into the layout by pulling from the top of the deck.

    On the next pages are a few layouts to get you started: Pick whichever one is best based on the question you're trying to answer! And keep in mind that when you first start doing readings it's TOTALLY normal to have no idea what's going on. *What should tarot feel like if I'm doing it right? How will I even know? Is there such a thing as doing it WRONG?* Pure magic; you won't; and definitely not.

    There are lots of cards to keep track of and you can't be expected to memorize every meaning and nuance. Which is why it's all about practice. Keep at it until it starts to make sense. Reading tarot is, in part, about finding your own voice and interpretations. I've shared the cards' long-accepted general meanings with you; now it's up to you to bring your own spin. If a Queen of Pentacles comes up with a Three of Cups and a Strength card, do your best to explain how they all interact based on who the reading is for and what the question is. If you feel like you're making it up, keep saying words and you'll eventually find your footing. I'm serious! Connect the dots, create meaning, and just go with it.

Now, if you're doing a reading and the drawn cards don't seem to match what the reading calls for—don't be surprised or thrown. Read on for a little guidance.

If a card's location in a reading is meant to be about a situation, event, or occurrence (like in the Year Ahead Spread on page 221) but a court card (aka a person card) is drawn, that could mean:

- a person with those characteristics may be coming into your life or a person with those characteristics already in your life may become more important
- YOU could be the person the card is referencing, meaning that kind of personality is one you should be learning from

- it's a warning to look out for someone with that personality

If a card's location in a reading is meant to be about a person (like #7 and #8 in the Celtic Cross Spread on page 226), but a situation card is pulled, that could mean:

- it's not the person ASKING the question who's got the problem reflected on the card—it's the situation being ASKED ABOUT that's problematic
- there's a problem at hand that has nothing to do with a person at all; you'll have to take a look at the entire reading to see what the tarot is trying to tell you

DAILY DRAW SPREAD

If you're looking for an easy way to practice, or for a quick sign, drawing one card each day is great. Go through the typical shuffling process while thinking about your day or a question that's on your mind. Pull a card from the top of the deck. That's your card of the day.

Good for: a quick check-in/direction for your day

THREE-CARD SPREAD

Use this reading for basic questions. Even though tarot can't predict the future, this spread will spotlight the important deets.

Good for: worries about upcoming presentations and parties

1. What happened in the past
2. What's happening now
3. What will happen soon

WHY YOU'RE AWESOME SPREAD

Use this spread when you need to remind yourself why you're so great.

Good for: when you need a pep talk

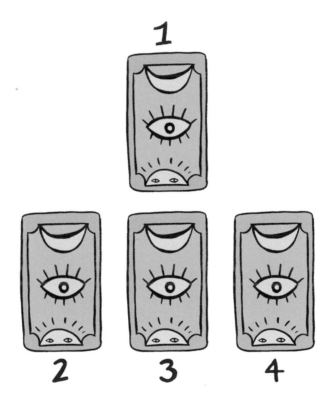

1. What you're best at
2. Why people respect you
3. What you can teach others
4. Your direction in life

THE YEAR AHEAD SPREAD

Use this reading to plan for the year ahead. Each card represents a season, so you can start this at any point in the year.

Good for: seeing what surprises are coming for you

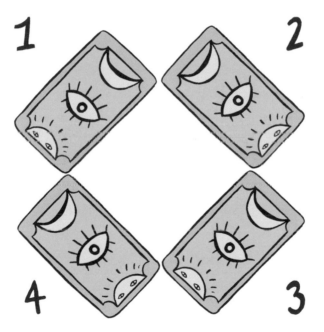

1. What will happen in spring for you
2. How summer will shake out
3. What to look for in fall
4. How you'll make it through winter

RELATIONSHIP SPREAD

Use this when you want to see how a relationship is going, for better or worse. Even when all your love interest texted back was a mysterious "K," this spread is here for you.

Good for: figuring out who feels what in a relationship, or if it will go somewhere

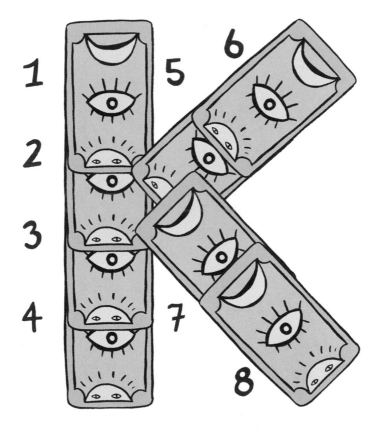

1. How you feel about relationships in general
2. How you feel about this person
3. How they feel about you
4. How this person feels about relationships in general
5. What you're worried about happening in this relationship
6. What you don't need to be worried about at all
7. How the relationship has been going so far
8. How the relationship will go in the future

GET OUT OF A SLUMP SPREAD

Use this reading for when you're feeling stuck/procrastinating.

Good for: when you have a major project due but can't get started

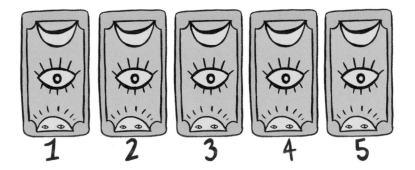

1. What's stopping you from getting this done
2. How you feel about this project
3. Something to focus on instead of thinking about being stuck
4. Why you should just get this done
5. How you'll feel once you finally do this

STAR SPREAD

Use this reading for when someone needs a way to recharge or refocus on their priorities.

Good for: deciding what subject to continue studying, solving fights with friends

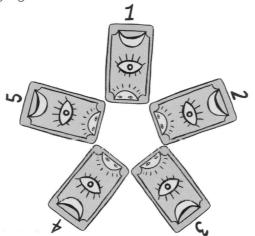

1. You right now (e.g., if you're feeling confident/sad/overworked/happy)
2. The task you need to get done (e.g., communicating better with friends/auditioning for the play/asking out your crush)
3. The challenges you're facing (e.g., your own thoughts holding you back/too many responsibilities)
4. Your personal strength (e.g., teamwork/keeping secrets/being charming)
5. The end result you're after (e.g., stability/friendship/achieving your goals)

CELTIC CROSS SPREAD

Use this reading for more complicated issues or more detailed questions. It will give you a bunch of background and guidance. Celtic Cross is a very traditional tarot spread, but don't be afraid of how many cards it calls for!

Good for: major life decisions, fully analyzing your crush/dating situation

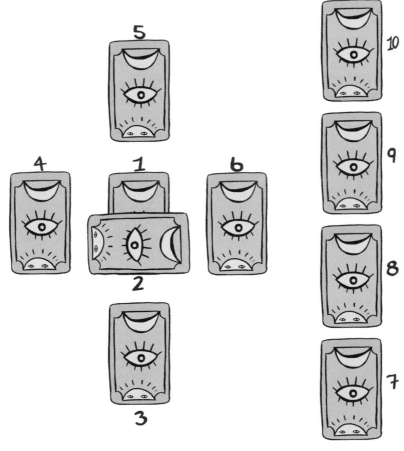

1. Your current state
2. Your main issue/problem
3. The heart of the matter at hand
4. Your past
5. What's important to you
6. What's coming
7. You
8. External influences
9. Your hopes AND your fears (sometimes you're afraid to hope for what you want)
10. Your future if you stay on this path

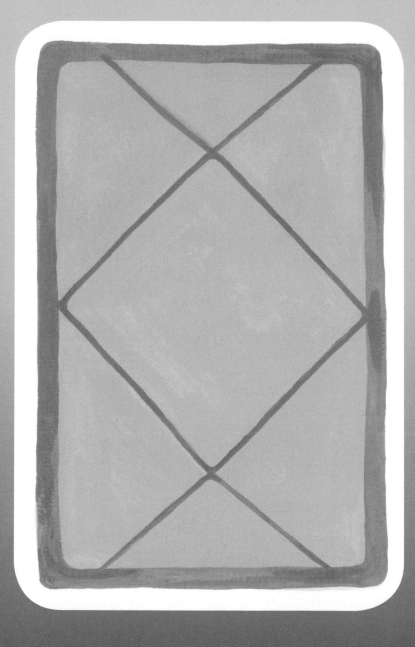

5

AND AWAY YOU GO!

Now that you've read through all the cards and the ways you can use them, start practicing! The more you lay the cards out and get familiar with their meanings, the easier it'll be to do readings.

Tapping into your intuition is a very powerful and useful tool. Soon you'll be able to trust your gut more because you'll be accustomed to seeing what it can do for you.

Reading tarot cards doesn't mean that you're a witch or that you practice black magic. As you've seen, it's a way to help interpret the world around us a little better. Some people look up their horoscopes immediately on the first day of any month; some people don't stop texting the group chat until they're sure they've gone over every possible outcome. For you, do what feels right! Maybe tarot can help bring some peace and calm into your world and the worlds of your friends.

We all could use a little more reassurance these days, especially as we come across bigger and bigger life decisions. Going into the world with your head high and your confidence up is important. Whatever you currently do that helps you hit your mojo, hopefully tarot can go in that tool belt, too.

Plus, reading tarot cards will help you feel secure with your choices and instincts. Everyone's style of reading is different based on personality. Maybe you prefer meditating before jumping into a reading, or maybe you need to dance around to get your mind off everything else. It's all accepted in tarot. Use those practices to grow comfortable with your own decision-making skills. Embrace your intuition and be proud of your gut feeling.

Everyone walks around the world with experiences and thoughts running through their heads that are wildly different from yours. Tarot, perhaps, can be a connecting thread that will help you understand your universe a little better and help you feel more connected to others.

ACKNOWLEDGMENTS FROM THE AUTHOR

Thank you, first of all, to all those showers you take when you're unemployed that give you mysterious sources of inspiration. Thank you, too, to Katie Heaney and her ability to respond to a text and email within minutes. It was through Katie that I was connected to the badass-est agent of all time, Allison Hunter, and through Allison that I was connected to Sara Sargent, a supreme editor with an eye for the woo-woo.

Kaelin Tully, thank you for reading early drafts of this book proposal and for being patient with texts from me that made me seem like some kind of crazed lifestyle magazine in grocery-store checkout lines.

Tamara Main, thank you for the equal amounts of support, patience, handholding, and full belief in me and this project. Thank you, also, for never laughing at any of my projects, unless they were supposed to be laughed at.

Thank you to Brioche, my cat (shut up), for walking all over my tarot cards any time they were out. Maybe your good, dumb energy rubbed off on them.

—S.M.

ACKNOWLEDGMENTS FROM THE ILLUSTRATOR

I would like to thank my twelve-year-old self for finding the new-age section of the public library. Without it I would never have discovered tarot. Also, I am very thankful for my amazing family and friends who were with me every step of the way. My deck started as a Kickstarter project and would not have been funded without the help of Joseph Shopen, Brenden Brown, Eric Zettlemoyer, Kevin Reidy, the tarot community, and all of your amazing contributions! Working on this project was a dream come true, and I am forever grateful and stoked to have been a part of this.

—M.D.L.P.